Morris Woodruff Seymour

A History of the Equestrian Statue of Israel Putnam

Morris Woodruff Seymour

A History of the Equestrian Statue of Israel Putnam

ISBN/EAN: 9783744726566

Printed in Europe, USA, Canada, Australia, Japan

Cover: Foto ©Suzi / pixelio.de

More available books at **www.hansebooks.com**

A HISTORY

OF THE

EQUESTRIAN STATUE

OF

ISRAEL PUTNAM,

AT BROOKLYN, CONN.

Reported to the General Assembly, 1889.

HARTFORD, CONN.:
PRESS OF THE CASE, LOCKWOOD & BRAINARD COMPANY.
1888.

CONTENTS.

PREFACE.

Although frequently suggested, it was not until the year 1886 that the State, by an official act, recognized its duty to erect a monument to the memory of ISRAEL PUTNAM.

In this year the Putnam Phalanx and the people of Windham County pressed the matter upon the attention of the General Assembly, and that body, after listening kindly to earnest memorials and the addresses of distinguished citizens, appointed by joint resolution commissioners to procure a monument to the memory of Gen. ISRAEL PUTNAM, and cause the same to be placed over his grave, in the town of Brooklyn, Conn.

This pleasant duty the commissioners have performed, and it is their purpose in the following pages to report to the General Assembly and to preserve for all who may be interested, an official account of their work and the exercises at the dedication of the monument.

> MORRIS W. SEYMOUR,
> HENRY C. ROBINSON,
> GEORGE G. SUMNER,
> GEORGE F. HOLCOMBE,
> HEMAN A. TYLER,
> GEORGE P. McLEAN.

ISRAEL PUTNAM.

(FROM A PAINTING BY H. I. THOMPSON).

RESOLUTIONS

CONCERNING

PUTNAM ❊ MONUMENT,

AND

REPORT OF COMMISSION

ACCEPTED BY THE GENERAL ASSEMBLY IN 1887.

RESOLUTION

CONCERNING MONUMENT AT THE GRAVE OF GENERAL ISRAEL PUTNAM, APPROVED FEBRUARY 19, 1886.

Resolved by this Assembly:

SECTION 1. That HENRY M. CLEVELAND of Brooklyn, HEMAN A. TYLER of Hartford, GEORGE F. HOLCOMBE of New Haven, GEORGE P. McLEAN of Simsbury, MORRIS W. SEYMOUR of Bridgeport, and HENRY C. ROBINSON and GEORGE G. SUMNER of Hartford, are hereby appointed a Commission to procure a monument to the memory of GENERAL ISRAEL PUTNAM, and cause the same to be placed over his grave in the town of Brooklyn.

SECTION 2. Said Commission is hereby authorized to make a contract in the name and in behalf of the State with some competent person to be by them selected for constructing said monument and placing it in position over said grave; provided that the expense to the State of said work shall be limited in said contract to a sum not exceeding ten thousand dollars.

REPORT OF COMMISSION

TO GENERAL ASSEMBLY, ACCEPTED, AND ORDERED ON
FILE IN THE OFFICE OF THE SECRETARY.

---

*To the General Assembly, State of Connecticut, January Session,
A.D. 1887 :*

The undersigned, having been appointed by the General
Assembly at its January Session, A.D. 1886, a Commission
to procure a monument to the memory of Major-General
Israel Putnam, and to erect the same over his remains in
the town of Brooklyn, in this State, as will more fully appear
by a copy of said act hereto annexed, would respectfully
report :

That immediately upon their said appointment, they met
at Hartford on the 19th day of February, and having duly
organized, unanimously adopted the following :

> *Voted,* To invite designs for a monument, to be erected in Brooklyn,
> Connecticut, to the memory of General Israel Putnam, said design to be
> submitted to the Secretary of the Commission, on or before the 15th of
> May, A.D. 1886. No restriction is made upon the nature, style, or
> character of the monument, except that its cost must not exceed the sum
> of ten thousand dollars. The Commission will allow the sum of two
> hundred and fifty dollars for any design they may choose to accept.

A large number of artists accepted this invitation, and
submitted designs according to the terms of said vote.
Some of them were exceedingly appropriate and meritorious.
As will be seen, no restrictions were made upon the nature
or style of the monument, and among the number submitted
was a design for an equestrian statue, which was so appropriate that the commission were of the opinion that if it
were possible to procure a monument of that character

within the sum appropriated, they ought so to do. They
therefore rejected all designs, as was their privilege, and
advertised for a further competition, limiting the same to
equestrian statues. At their second competition, four
designs of exceptional merit were submitted, one by Mr. E.
S. Woods of Hartford, one by Mr. George E. Bissell of
Poughkeepsie, N. Y., one by the Bridgeport Monumental
Bronze Company, and a fourth by Mr. Karl Gerhardt of
Hartford. After several days of very careful study and consideration, the committee made selection of the design presented by Mr. Gerhardt, and voted him the two hundred and
fifty dollars award. They subsequently, on the second day
of October, A.D. 1886, entered into a contract with him to
erect a monument modeled on that design, on the site
selected by the Commission, for the sum of nine thousand
seven hundred and fifty dollars. The names of the artists
who so kindly submitted their designs to the commission
are hereto annexed, as also a copy of the contract entered
into with Mr. Gerhardt.

The act of the General Assembly requires that the monument should be erected in the town of Brooklyn in this
State, and "over the grave" of the General. A literal com-
pliance with this direction, if the act was to be interpreted
to mean over the grave where the General was originally
buried, was found to be impossible, as even the simplest
monument in that place would have interfered with the right
of others in a manner in which the Commission had neither
the power nor the inclination to do. Upon this fact being
brought to the attention of the descendants of General
Putnam, they acting through and by the Hon. Wm. H. Putnam, a lineal descendant of the General, immediately signi-
fied their willingness to remove his remains to such place as
the Commission might select, so that the monument when
erected should, in fact, stand over his grave; and this too
without any expense to the State. As they had the legal
right to make such removal, the Commission could see no
objection to such course.

In the matter of selecting the site, the Commission here had a great deal of trouble, and have been compelled to hold a large number of meetings. The public square in the village of Brooklyn belongs to the First Unitarian Society, but upon such terms and conditions that the Society was not willing that the monument should be erected or the interment made at that place lest their title to such property might be endangered. A public spirited citizen of the town tried to purchase the lot upon which the house of General Putnam stood, in order to present it to the State, as a site for the monument, but as he was unable so to do, the Commission finally selected the location a few rods below the public square. It is on the northeast corner of the historic Mortlake property. To the north is the old church, where Putnam rang the bell and attended service; to the northeast, near the site of his inn, stand the remains of the tree on which hung the tavern sign; to the east, the field where the old hero left his plow and the quiet pursuits of husbandry, for the cause of liberty and the field of battle. To this place the descendants of General Putnam have removed his remains, and placing them in a sarcophagus they have been built.into the foundation upon which the statue will ultimately rest. In its work the Commission has been greatly assisted by the untiring energy, kindness, and generosity of the Hon. Thomas S. Marlor. He not only donated to the State the plot of ground upon which the monument will stand, but graded the same, paved and erected a granite roadway and coping around it. The town of Brooklyn, at a legal meeting warned for that purpose, generously voted the sum of five hundred dollars, which has enabled the Commission to carry on its work and pay the necessary expenses of advertising, etc.

It is hoped and expected that the monument will be ready to be delivered over to the State during the early part of the coming Summer, complete and paid for, within the amount appropriated. Every effort will be made to accomplish this result by the 17th of June.

2

It would be fitting that this event should be celebrated in a manner worthy of the memory of Connecticut's greatest revolutionary hero, and of the dignity of the State. If it should seem best to your Honorable Body that the State should take part in the ceremonies incident to the unveiling, presentation, and acceptance of this work of art, which we trust and believe will be a fitting tribute on the part of a grateful people to one who gave his all for American independence, it will be necessary for you to take into consideration some bill directing the manner of, and providing the means for such ceremony. All of which is respectfully submitted.

On behalf of the Committee,

MORRIS W. SEYMOUR,
HEMAN A. TYLER.

LIST OF COMPETITORS FOR THE PUTNAM MONUMENT DESIGN.

No. 1. John Bishop, New London, Conn.
No. 2. Charles Conrad, Hartford, Conn.
No. 3. Berkshire Marble Company, Boston, Mass.
No. 4. Karl Gerhardt, Hartford, Conn.
No. 5. S. Maslen & Company, Hartford, Conn.
No. 6. John Baptista, Chelsea, Mass.
No. 7. William Booth, New London, Conn.
No. 8. Calvin S. Davis, Waterford, Conn.
No. 9. Charles F. Stoll, New London, Conn.
No. 10. Thomas W. Casey, New London, Conn.
No. 11. Alfred F. Stoll, New London, Conn.
No. 12. George E. Bissell, Poughkeepsie, N. Y.
No. 13. Andrew O'Connor, Worcester, Mass.
No. 14. Simonson & Poll, Washington, D. C.
No. 15. White Bronze Company, Bridgeport, Conn.
No. 16. R. L. Pierson, Park Place, New York.
No. 17. George Keller, Hartford, Conn.
No. 18. Enoch S. Woods, Hartford, Conn. ·
No. 19. Smith Granite Company, Providence, R. I.
No. 20. John Reicther, Hartford, Conn.

No. 21. Alexander Doyle, Great Jones St., New York.
No. 22. C. S. Luce, West 23d Street, New York.
No. 23. New England Granite Co., 1321 Broadway, N. Y.
No. 24. George Crabtree, New Britain, Conn.
No. 25. John Hannah, New Britain, Conn.
No. 26. Brunner & Tryon, Union Square, New York.

SECOND COMPETITION.

Enoch S. Woods, Hartford, Conn.
George E. Bissell, Poughkeepsie, N. Y.
Karl Gerhardt, Hartford, Conn.
Bridgeport Monumental Bronze Company, Bridgeport, Conn.
Andrew O'Connor, Worcester, Mass.

CONTRACT WITH KARL GERHARDT.

This agreement made and entered into this second day of October, A.D. 1886, by and between the State of Connecticut (by its agents undersigned) of the first part, and Karl Gerhardt . of Hartford, Connecticut, of the second part, witnesseth as follows:

Said Gerhardt hereby agrees to make a bronze equestrian statue of Israel Putnam, granite or other stone pedestal, in accordance with specifications hereunto appended.

And said Gerhardt agrees that he will execute all said work with his best skill and ability, and that he will submit to the inspection and approval of said agents his design and studies of any and every part of said work, and will conform to their express wishes in fashioning and constructing the same.

And the said Gerhardt agrees to complete the same to the acceptance and approval of said Commission on or before the first day October, 1887, absolutely, and on or before June 1, 1887, if possible.

And said party of the first part, agrees upon the full and complete performance of said undertaking by said Gerhardt, as hereinbefore set forth, to pay to him the sum of ($9,750) nine thousand seven hundred and fifty dollars.

Specifications of Equestrian Statue of Israel Putnam with pedestal and foundation, to be made for the State of Connecticut by Karl Gerhardt.

Statue and pedestal to be made after the style of the design accepted by the Putnam Monument Commission, subject to alterations to be made by said Commission, which alterations are to be made in all cases without extra charge by said Gerhardt.

The statue and pedestal together to be twenty-five feet in height, divided as follows : the statue to be twelve feet in height; pedestal to be thirteen feet in height.

The statue to be composed of the best bronze, finished in workmanlike manner, and chemically colored.

The pedestal to be of granite, or other stone, its character, whether Westerly, Quincy, or other granite, or freestone or other stone, to be determined by the Commission.

Stones to be used in pedestal to be of dimensions, and to be dressed as prescribed by said Commission, and all to be pure, homogeneous, and free from white horse or other defect.

If said pedestal shall be built of freestone, it shall be subjected to such treatment as said Commission may prescribe, and each stone therein contained shall be accepted by said agents of the State.

Said pedestal shall have a bronze frieze of oak and laurel leaves encircling the cap stones to tablets, to be made of the best bronze in workmanlike manner and chemically colored.

Tablets are to be made on each side running from capstone to platform which forms part of base of pedestal, and said tablets are to bear the original inscription of General Putnam's tombstone, written by President Dwight of Yale College, the same to be cut on the surface of the tablets.

On either end of said pedestal there shall be an ornamental wolf's head, composed of best bronze, finished in workmanlike manner, and chemically colored, and forming a division of seats. Said pedestal to be built after the design accepted by said Commission.

The base stones of said pedestal are to be twenty-two feet and six inches in length, twelve feet and six inches in width, and twelve inches in depth. Upon said stones and surrounding the base of the pedestal is to be erected a granite seat, one and one-half feet in height, to be completed after the manner of said design. Foundation to be laid to the acceptance of said Commission, in all respects, as to depth, size, quality, and dressing of stone, character of material, and workmanship.

The same to be built in the town of Brooklyn, Connecticut, in such place as said agents shall designate, and said pedestal and statue are to be placed thereon by said Gerhardt.

All of said undertakings by said Gerhardt are to be done to the acceptance and approval of said Commission.

KARL GERHARDT.

HENRY M. CLEVELAND,
HEMAN A. TYLER,
GEORGE P. McLEAN,
MORRIS W. SEYMOUR,
HENRY C. ROBINSON,
GEORGE G. SUMNER.
By HEMAN A. TYLER,
Secretary.
Hereunto authorized.

The form of the foregoing contract is approved by us.

HENRY C. ROBINSON,
GEO. P. McLEAN,
HEMAN A. TYLER,
GEORGE G. SUMNER.

HARTFORD, October 2, 1886.

WARRANTEE DEED EXECUTED BY THOMAS S. MARLOR.

To all people to whom these presents shall come, GREETING :

Know ye that I, Thomas S. Marlor of the town of Brooklyn, County of Windham, and State of Connecticut, for the consideration of One Dollar received to my full satisfaction of the State of Connecticut, do give, grant, bargain, sell, and confirm, unto the said State of Connecticut one certain tract of land situated in said town of Brooklyn, bounded and described as follows, to wit : Beginning at the southeast corner of said tract, at a stone post, thence north 8¼° east 64 feet 6 inches, bounded easterly by the highway leading from Brooklyn to Plainfield, thence north 79°, west 78 feet, bounded north on land of the First Trinitarian Society, thence south 10°, west 66 feet 3 inches, bounded west on land of said grantor, thence south 80°, east 80 feet to first-mentioned point. It is understood and agreed that the above-described piece of land is to be used for a site for a monument to be erected to the memory of General Israel Putnam.

To have and to hold the above-granted and bargained premises, with the appurtenances thereof, unto said State, its successors and assigns forever, to it and their own proper use and behoof. And also, I, the said grantor, do for myself, my heirs, executors, and administrators, covenant with the said State, its successors and assigns, that at and until the ensealing of these presents, I am well seized of the premises as a good, indefeasible estate in fee simple, and have good right to bargain and sell the same in manner and form as is above written; and that the same is free from all incumbrances whatsoever. And the said grantor by these presents binds himself, and his heirs, and assigns forever, that no building shall be erected further east than at present standing on land of said grantor adjoining.

And furthermore, I, the said grantor, do, by these presents, bind myself and my heirs forever to warrant and defend the above-granted and bargained premises to said State and its successors and assigns, against all claims and demands whatsoever.

WARRANTY DEED EXECUTED BY THOMAS S. MARLOR.

To all people to whom these presents shall come, GREETING :

Know ye that I, Thomas S. Marlor of the town of Brooklyn, County of Windham, and State of Connecticut, for the consideration of One Dollar received to my full satisfaction of the State of Connecticut, do give, grant, bargain, sell, and confirm unto the said State of Connecticut, certain land situated in said Brooklyn, and described as follows, to wit : A certain driveway situated on the south side of property deeded by this grantor to the State by deed dated September 10, 1886, and recorded in Brooklyn Land Records, Vol. xiii, page 78. Said way being sixteen (16) feet wide, and bounded north on land of the State, east by highway, south by the Mortlake Hotel property, so called, and west by said Mortlake Hotel property, extending seventy feet in length, more or less.

The said Marlor, grantor, hereby reserving to himself, his heirs, and assigns, a right of way over the land herein conveyed, said right to include all privileges of ingress and egress which may be necessary to the use and enjoyment of the said Mortlake Hotel property.

To have and to hold the above-granted and bargained premises, with the appurtenances thereof, unto the said State, its successors and assigns forever, to it and their own proper use and behoof.

And also I, the said grantor, do for myself, my heirs, executors, and administrators, covenant with the said State, its successors, heirs, and assigns, that at and until the ensealing of these presents, I am well seized of the premises, as a good, indefeasible estate in fee simple, and have good right to bargain and sell the same in manner and form as is above *written;* and that the same is free from all incumbrances whatsoever, except as above stated.

And furthermore, I, the said grantor, do by these presents bind myself and my heirs forever to warrant and defend the above-granted and bargained premises to the said State, its successors and assigns, against all claims and demands whatsoever, except as above stated.

NOTE.—The specifications for Pedestal as also the report of Commissioner Henry M. Cleveland, disapproving of the action of his associates in approving the site, will be found in Legislative Documents, 1887.

RESOLUTION

PROVIDING FOR DEDICATION OF MONUMENT, APPROVED MAY 10, 1887.

Resolved by this Assembly:

That His Excellency, the governor of this State, be requested to call out at least one regiment of the Connecticut National Guard to assist at and participate in the dedication of the Monument erected by the State to the memory of Major-General Israel Putnam.

That the Quartermaster-General of the State be, and he is hereby, authorized and directed to furnish, erect, and remove such tents and camp equipage, and fire such salutes as the Commission appointed to erect said monument may require on the occasion of such dedication.

That a sum not exceeding six thousand five hundred dollars be and is hereby appropriated to defray the expenses which may be incurred by the said Commissioners in the ceremonies attending the dedication of said monument, and that the comptroller be directed to draw his order on the treasurer of the State for such portions of said sum as may be called for by the chairman of said Commission and approved by the Governor.

NOTE,— The words "and approved by the Governor" were added by subsequent resolution adopted May 19, 1887.

RESOLUTION

ADOPTED BY THE TOWN OF BROOKLYN APPOINTING
COMMITTEE TO AID COMMISSION.

"*Resolved*, That a committee of fifty (50) be appointed for
the town to act in harmony with the wishes of the Putnam Monument Commission in the dedicatory services of the proposed
Putnam Monument, consisting of the following gentlemen :

BENJAMIN A. BAILEY,
WILLIAM H. PUTNAM,
THOMAS S. MARLOR,
WILLIAM CLAPP,
STEPHEN H. TRIPP,
ENOS L. PRESTON,
THEODORE D. POND,
REV. THOMAS FOGG,
CHARLES B. WHEATLEY,
WILLIAM H. CUTLER,
REV. E. S. BEARD,
CHARLES PHILLIPS,
REV. G. W. BREWSTER,
HENRY H. GREEN,
HASCHAEL F. COX,
CHARLES G. WILLIAMS,
JOHN G. POTTER,
SAMUEL BRADFORD,
VINE R. FRANKLIN,
AMOS KENDALL,
CHARLES SEARLS,
ALBERT DAY,
L. S. ATWOOD,
REV. S. F. JARVIS,
FRANK E. BAKER,

JOHN M. BROWN,
REV. WILLIAM GUSSMAN.
JOHN HYDE,
DARIUS DAY,
HENRY S. MARLOR, JR.
REV. A. J. CULP,
JOHN N. BURDICK,
GEORGE BROWN,
ELIAS H. MAIN,
JAMES C. PALMER,
SIMON SHEPARD,
ALBERT D. PUTNAM,
EDWIN SCARBOROUGH,
JOSEPH B. STETSON,
THOMAS R. BAXTER,
WILLARD DAY,
FRANK DAY,
CHARLES H. CORNWALL,
EPHRAIM PRENTICE,
RUSSELL W. BAILEY,
WILLIS A. KENYON,
DANIEL B. HATCH,
J. SPRAGUE BARD,
WELLINGTON E. JAMES,
JOHN A. SHARPE,

A true copy,

Attest,   THEO. D. POND,
Chairman.

3

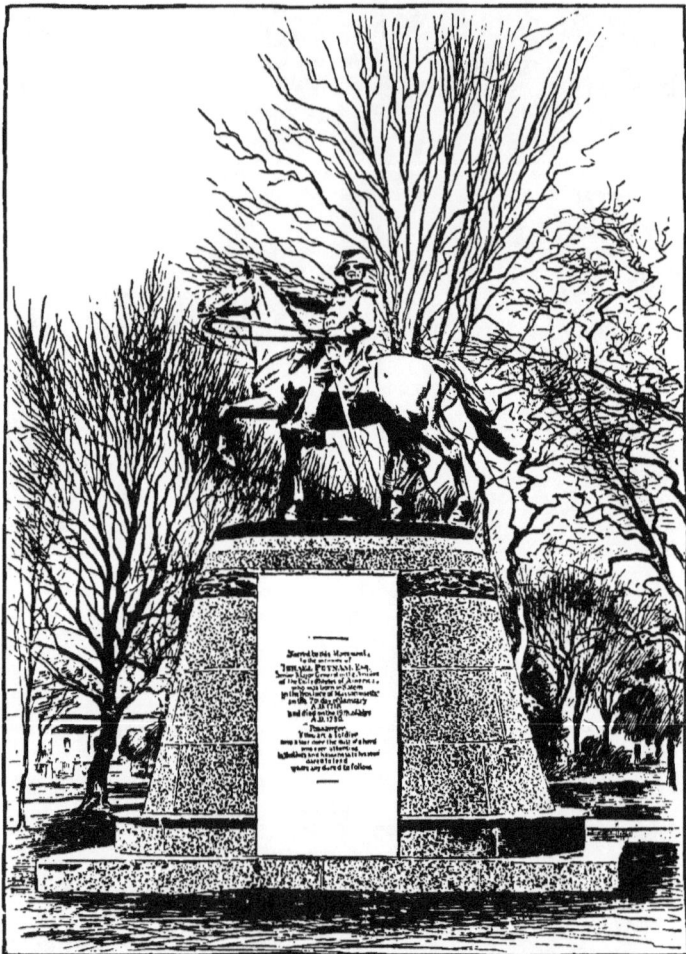

EQUESTRIAN STATUE OF ISRAEL PUTNAM
AT BROOKLYN, CONNECTICUT.

EXERCISES AT DEDICATION

OF

EQUESTRIAN ❊ STATUE,

JUNE 14, 1888.

PRESENTATION ADDRESS.

MORRIS W. SEYMOUR.

Fellow-Citizens, Ladies and Gentlemen:

A neglected grave, a battered and broken tomb-stone and underneath the bones of a hero:—this the picture which inspired the good people of this town with the desire to erect a more fitting memorial to one of their most distinguished fellow townsmen. This inspiration spreading, as all good inspirations must, into the adjoining towns and throughout the length and breadth of the county, at last made itself felt in the hall of legislation, and in 1886-7, the State of Connecticut, ever mindful of the reputation of her children, appropriated a sum of money and appointed a commission to erect and appropriately dedicate a monument to one of her noblest sons. Their work done, that commission here present to your excellency, as the official head of the State and the representative of its people, the fruits of their labor. On yonder plot of ground, the property of the State, the gift of a generous citizen of this town, wrapped about by that flag which he did so much to elevate among the nations of the earth—chiseled by the hand of cunning artists in bronze and granite, stands the statue of one who in life was simple as a child, tender as a woman, brave as a lion, and underneath that statue rest the remains of Israel Putnam.

GOVERNOR LOUNSBURY'S ADDRESS OF ACCEPTANCE.

In accepting this Statue in the name of the State I give voice to the thanks of this Commonwealth for the faithful services of the Commissioners and for the admirable work of the artist.

We all know that we can do nothing here to-day to perpetuate the memory of the illustrious dead. He, whose command directed and whose presence inspired the heroic struggle on Bunker Hill, crowns with his glory even the lofty monument that is erected there. The genius of neither orator nor artist can gild the fame of Israel Putnam.

You place this monument not so much as a duty which you owe to the dead, as a duty which you owe to yourselves. It is alike the outburst and the token of your love and gratitude. It is not to mark the mortal dust of the immortal soldier, but it is rather to point your children to his living example, to the teachings which he chiseled on the monuments of a Nation's history.

It is alike well whether we celebrate this hour in the throb and glow of a generous state pride, or whether, forgetting that we have any share in Putnam's glory, we seek to impress upon our hearts the simple and sublime lesson of his life.

Israel Putnam was great in his energy, great in his courage, great in his patriotism, but he was greatest of all in his intense personality. It was a rugged personality, but it so stamped its influence upon the men of his time and upon the time itself, that, next to Washington, no soldier of the Revolution left behind him a grander work or one more sharply defined as his own. His tireless activity and his matchless courage were not simply the results of splendid physical gifts, but they were rather parts themselves of a mighty soul so intense in its unborn energy that it knew no weariness; so consecrated to its work that it knew no fear.

Putnam was a patriot of the patriots, but to one of his profound individuality, patriotism meant something more than its simple definition in the schools. What we call Putnam's patriotism was this generous passion intensified and directed by his obedience to the two great laws of his nature. His manhood, asserting the right to its own development as the supreme end of its existence and demanding civil liberty as the sacred means to this sacred end, was the first great law. And it was supplemented by a second, written in the surpassing generosity of his nature: The right which thou claimest for thyself and which thou shalt not basely yield is thy brother's also, and in thy equal love for him thou shalt struggle for thy brother's right as thou strugglest for thine own.

Always and everywhere it is man's intelligent obedience to these two laws of his higher nature that gives to patriotism all its worth that makes it a factor in civilization and progress. Love for fellow man, appreciation of one's self, faith in one's destiny, a clear perception of the right means of development, all alike lie at the base of its virtue and power, and he who by his teachings or his life lessens the force of any one of these essentials degrades the individual and undermines the State.

The sturdy self-asserting manhood and the unselfish devotion of Putnam and of the men cast in his heroic mold won for them and bequeathed to you the blessings of constitutional liberty. It remains for you through the same virtues to preserve these blessings for yourselves and to transmit them to the generations to come. To do this you need no special school in which to teach the duty of patriotism. Least of all do you need to inculcate the doctrine that the State is above the citizen. The State may be divinely appointed but in the State itself there is no divinity. Upon the individual alone God has stamped his own immortal image. Set the destiny of the State above the destiny of the individual and you found your government upon a falsehood, upon sand that the storm of discontent and floods of revolution will surely sweep away. But fill the soul with just conceptions of its own immortal destiny, educate the mind until it clearly sees the need of civil liberty to man's development and the need of the State to the preservation of that liberty and the people will protect the Government as they protect themselves. Do this and you found the State upon a rock so firm that it will stand while God's truth upon the earth endures.

POEM

BY PROFESSOR CHARLES F. JOHNSON, TRINITY COLLEGE, HARTFORD.

The men of Rome, who framed the first free state,
When Rome in men and not in wealth was great,
Placed in their homes, as in an honored shrine,
Rude portrait busts, cut with no art divine,
But roughly chipped from rock or wrought in brass
By craftsmen of the town; so might time pass,
And still the worthy sire perpetuate
Brave thoughts, brave deeds, in men of later date.
And these they called their household gods, and knew
Them worthy worship, and from them they drew
The consciousness that men had lived and died
In days agone; these dull and heavy-eyed
Stone faces mutely testified that life
Is grounded in the past, that toil and strife
Are not for self, nor borne for self alone,
That children reap where worthy sires have sown.

'Twas thus the Julian or the Fabian name
Linked past to present in ancestral fame;
And thus the Roman gens inherited
Traditions from the past, life from the dead, —
A life, not fleeting with the life of man,
But life, renewed, continuing, whose span
Binds men in generations by a law
Higher than that through which the living draw
To living comrades and to present friends,
A law of higher sanction, higher ends,
Because it is a law beyond our ken,
Binding, not man to man, but man to men.

But there were those who had been called to die
When Roman legions marched to victory,

4

Who reached the higher plane of citizen,
Where nobler bonds made one all Roman men,
Who served that august thing, the Roman state,
And held their gens, their homes, subordinate.
These men the Romans honored over all,
Their busts were placed for a memorial
About the forum, where all men could see
The great republic's honored ancestry;
For them the white and flawless stone was brought,
For them the precious silver bronze was wrought
By one whose cunning hand could realize
In bronze or stone the broader sympathies,
Who had that feeling for the soul of man
Which makes an artist of an artisan.

Often on festal days the father led
His sons up to the Capitol, and said,
" Look ; this is Fabius, whose constancy,
Unshaken in defeat, saved Italy
From Hannibal ; your grandsire served with him
In those dark days when all our hope grew dim ;
This is that elder, greater one with whom
Your grandsire's grandsire fighting died when Rome
Conquered the Samnite hordes — Cincinnatus,
We have not now such men to fight for us ;
And this is he, the greater, mightier far,
' Who, born no king, made monarchs draw his car ' ;
And this is Regulus, who kept his faith
With Carthaginian foes — though faith meant death
He would not break his word ; beneath is graved
' He lost his life, but Roman honor saved.'
Alas, this modern age can never breed
Men of the pith of these, our honored dead."

Thus would the veteran to his children praise
The patriot heroes of the ancient days ;
Thus were preserved the annals of the state,
And, thus, the civic virtues, incarnate
In brass or stone, kept life, grew broad, and were
The compact base of Roman character.

We, too, have our great names.   How shall we set
These jewels in Columbia's coronet?
Where shall we place our heroes,— we who owe
More to our dead than they of long ago?
They tore the feudal shackles from the state,
And built an England here regenerate
By sacrifice and blood, and by their deed
Enforced and supplemented Runnymede;
They saved the great tradition of the race,
Defiled or lost in its old dwelling place,—
The folk-moot and the witenagemote, —
Of freedom's tree the deep earth-holding root.
Through them we teach the world what freedom means;
It is our heritage, but others' dreams;
It has no center here, the soil is free;
There is no cloistered shrine for liberty.
For Greene, for Putnam, or for Washington
We need no Abbey and no Pantheon.
They fought not to exalt a conquering race
·But for mankind; their pedestal and place
Is underneath the over-arching sky,
Our dome of state is God's own canopy.
Erect in Nature's presence let them stand,
The free-born heroes of our Yankee land!
Strong-limbed, great-hearted men of massive mould,
There is no marble white enough, nor gold
Of fineness fit to build their monument;
No roof is needed but the heavens bent
Above their heads, — the air, wide-spread and free,
Shall symbolize a people's liberty.

The labored fabric of scholastic rhyme
Seems inharmonious with this place and time;
Rough, flinty shards of Saxon speech were fit
For Putnam's name, to rightly honor it.
His memory needs no set and garnished phrase,
His deeds are made no greater by our praise; .
We were the losers if tradition dim
Were all that kept alive the thought of him,
The brave old man and true, who set his face
Like rock, towards liberty's abiding place.

Like Abraham Lincoln's and John Brown's, his name
Old English half, half from the Bible came;
His rugged Saxon nature held, like theirs,
Two kindred elements; the one which dares
To act; the other, higher one, which hears
The murmur of a people's voice, and fears
Not to respond with action, though slow years
May come and go and never realize
God's high commission to the centuries.
They feel the ground-swell of some sea beyond,
The deep pulsation of the vast profound;
The great communal heart beats in their breast;
Unspoken sympathies forbid them rest, —
These tribunes of the people, they who trace
Their lineage back to men of that free race
Which in its home beside the Northern sea
Laid the broad basis of democracy.

Thus Putnam felt at once our cause was right,
And tarried not to think of England's might.
The ragged Continental uniform
Was freedom's chosen livery, when 'twas worn
By men like him.   No labored argument
On policy or law framed his intent.
Bluff, hearty, simple, cheerful, resolute,
A firm-set soul, torn by no subtle doubt,
By birth and nurture he was formed a man
Fit for the time, great freedom's partizan.

In Putnam's youth, each frontier settlement
Was like the vanguard of an army, sent
To hold the outposts.   In that rugged school
Tempered and trained, he proved a man to rule
The rude frontiersman, for he "dared to lead
Where any dared to follow."   In their need
Men looked to him.   In God's appointed hour
Our war for freemen's rights against the power
Imposed on Englishmen in their old home, —
Which still by impotence avoids its doom, —
Our war for civic independence came.

A tower of strength was Israel Putnam's name,
A rallying-word for patriot acclaim ; —
It meant resolve, and hope, and bravery,
And steady cheerfulness, and constancy.

A free state needs no death's-head for a sign
Of sovereignty ; it is itself divine.
Weak simulacra of old feudal things,
Bourbon or Guelph,—fantastic, out-worn kings,—
Are hateful to it.   Slow its instinct draws
Unto its champions, by those deep laws
In which its being rests.   It knows the soul
In which its own is mirrored; then the whole
Moves as a whole.   Voices as one voice ring,—
"The man! the man!   Behold the freeman's king!"

God sends our kings, Lincoln and Washington ;
Putnam is not of these.   They stand alone,
And solitary on their heights remain ;
He with his fellows on a lower plane.
But on that plane of broad humanity,
What stronger man or nobler soul than he —
A nature on broad lines and simple plan,
Type of the primitive American !

We will not smile as did the "gilded youth,"
Nor make a sun-myth of his "old she-wolf,"
Like some poor pedants of these later years,
Who, lacking insight, claiming to be seers,
Hungry for slander as their daily food,
Moth-eat the fame of all our "great and good" ; —
(When such men die they'll find 'twill be as well
To avoid the ghost of Uncle Israel —)
We know the man too well to laugh, unless
In love — he is too big.   Perhaps in dress
Or speech he was uncouth ; perhaps his pen
Ran to phonetic forms of words.   What then !
Give him a horse and sword, and everywhere
The enemy advance, "Old Put" is *there*.
He had a knack of getting in the way

And getting out in time. The British say
He all that Jersey winter hardly would
Allow them leisure time to cook their food ;
For just as they were sitting down at table
They'd hear a noise, and that "abominable,
Ubiquitous, old, rebel general "
Would make an unexpected morning call,
And "cook their goose " himself, with Yankee sauce,
And then, with prisoners and spoils, be off.
Our other generals might be there, or here ;
On right or left, or hurrying from the rear,
But Putnam and his men were always *near.*
His instinct taught him where his men should go
To capture trains and squadrons of the foe;
Toil could not daunt him nor his age forbid,
The more he had to do the more he did.
Though three-score years and one, his zeal outran
The energy of many a younger man,
And, had his years been more by ten per cent.,
He would have filled a good-sized continent.

Such were our Continentals, such the one
Called on to lay a nation's corner-stone.
To found a nation needs a man to act,
A man whose thought is welded close to fact.
For, though the essential basis of the State
Is laid by elders, who in grave debate
Search precedent and history, and draw
From philosophic fount the organic law,
Great is the man who strikes, strikes for the right
By that sure instinct which sees more than sight.
Without the soldier's arm, state-craft is vain,
If force invade men's rights, force must maintain ;
A people's uplift martyrs' lives demands ;
Rooted in conflict all man's progress stands,
And through all time this truth has firmly stood,
A nation's corner-stone is laid in blood.
Our corner-stone was laid on Bunker Hill,
And Israel Putnam laid it. 'Twas his will
Inspired, his dauntless energy upheld

Our farmer-soldiers on that fateful field.
Years were summed up in that æonian day
When Putnam's shout rang o'er the furious fray
The battle-cry of freedom, — all who heard,
To battle-fury felt their pulses stirred.
It rings across the years, its music is
Accordant with the cheer from Salamis
Or Marathon, or with Rienzi's cry:
"The people's rights, and death to tyranny."

———

And, if in years to come men should forget
That only freedom makes a nation great ;
If in the turmoil of this modern world,
Where hopes and faiths, together heaped and hurled,
Obscure the visage of our father's God,
And make us recreant to our Saxon blood ;
If men grow less as wealth accumulates,
Till gold becomes the life-blood of our States ;
If swarms of European outcasts come
. To poison freedom in her latest home, —
The socialists, who know no social laws,
The communists, foes to the common cause ; —
If all our country seems degenerate,
Our great republic, heir to common fate,
Till some give up the duties of a man,
Forfeit their birthright as American ;
Should all these heavy ills weigh down our heart,
We'll turn to him who acted well his part
In those old days, draw lessons from his fame,
And hope and courage from his honored name.

But should the anarch's red flag be unfurled
In some great city of our western world,
If, some time, hand to hand and face to face,
Men meet those "enemies of the human race,"
We'll call upon the spirit of "Old Put,"
The farmer-soldier of Connecticut,
As they of yore.   We should not call in vain ;
From distant prairie and from western plain,
From Lake Ontario unto Puget Sound,

Where're the good old Yankee stock is found,
We'd have reply : " Our sturdy fathers fought
For civil rights, and won ; these are inwrought
Deep in our hearts. We hold our lives in fee
To keep unsmirched that precious legacy.
Strike that old drum once more, and you shall see
New 'Minute men,' and 'Sons of liberty.' "

Our noblemen were not mere dukes of shires ;
Kings without crowns, the continent was theirs.
Therefore, to-day we know no boundaries ;
No north no south confines our sympathies,
Nor east nor west ; our country's reveillé
Calls forth an uncontracted loyalty.
This was a patriot in no narrow sense,
Let our whole country do him reverence.

This monument, by skillful artist wrought,
Sums up and formulates a people's thought,
Else vague or lost, and renders permanent
The only deathless thing, a sentiment.
With democratic dignity instinct,
To memories of freedom's battles linked,
'Tis set a beacon in this ancient town.
'Twill stand when we are gone, and long hand down
The light of liberty in this her home.
In future years may children's children come
As to a sacred spot, to look upon
The rugged face of freedom's champion.
So may Columbia's empire ever be
Land of the free brave — home of the brave free.

MEMORIAL ADDRESS.

HENRY C. ROBINSON.

Ninety-eight years ago the wasted form of an old soldier, scarred by tomahawk and bullet, was laid to rest in yonder graveyard. The sacred acres were filled with mourners. He was consigned to sleep in the echoes of artillery and of musketry, and under the glories of the flag, the fibres of whose folds his own brave hands had so conspicuously helped to weave. His epitaph was written by the foremost scholar of our State. The fret of time, the frost of winter, and the selfish hand of the relic-hunter wasted the stone slab on which it was written. And here, above a handful of ashes, all that remains of that stalwart frame, which, in life, was the inspiration of Colonists, the hate of Frenchmen, the fear of Englishmen, and the awe of Indians, to-day, late, but not too late, a grateful State has built a seemly and enduring pedestal, has placed upon it his war-horse, and called again to his saddle, with his bronzed features saluting the morning, the Connecticut hero of the revolution.

Blessed is a state which has a history. Its present is the natural evolution of its past. Out of struggles it has grown; from storms and sunlight of other years it has made strength. Its greatness of other centuries is its renewed and transfigured greatness of to-day, its traditions are its inspirations, its buried

5

heroes are its living prophets. It is the blessedness
of continued personality, the manliness of the mature
man; its brain has developed with its muscles, its
heart with its bones. Reverence and pride for the
past, the kindling warmth of tender associations, and
the hallowed flames of love are its attributes. The
scholar reads about it, the poet sings of it, the phi-
losopher studies it. The banks of its streams are
sacred for the foot-prints upon them; its mountains
are dear for the brave steps that climbed them; its
groves are instinct with the meditations of its patriot
fathers; its churches are pure with the purity of its
saints; its graveyards are peopled with the presences of
its ancestry. Thermopylæ was a perpetual legacy to
the sons of Sparta, the atmosphere of the Academy
was an everlasting inheritance to the men of Athens.
The children of Israel sing the songs of Miriam and
David, study the philosophy of Moses, and Ezra, and
Hillel, fight over the battles of Saul and the Macca-
bees, and rightly say, they are all ours. The wars
are over, the wisdom is written, the lyrics are sung,
the laws are written on papyrus, are cut in stone, are
printed on paper, but the lesson in them all is as
fresh as a bubbling spring. We stand almost aghast
before the grandeur of a new state, as Dakota,
but we find no leaves of history to turn over
and study and ponder. But when we examine
the record of the last two and a half centuries
of human progress, the filial love of the people
of Connecticut finds a catalogue of statesmen,
and warriors, and orators, and philanthropists, a
story of patriotism, and self-government, and education, and discipline, and virtue, and piety, better

than all the traditions, gathered from three thousand years, which haunt the waters of the Ganges, or are assembled on the banks of the Nile. And the result of those early frictions and fights with rough nature and rougher man are written in the culture, and courage, and refinement, and sentiment of our little Commonwealth of to-day. There was choice seed dropped in the scant" soil of the wilderness by the pilgrims and by the colonial rebels, but lo, the wilderness has become a garden and blossoms like the rose.

A nation's character may be read in its heroes. It has been often said that no nation is better than its gods. Nor can it be unlike its demi-gods. Tell us what were the shrines in the Pantheon and whose ashes lie in Westminster Abbey, and we can more than guess what was Rome and what is England. And if the gates of the abbeys have opened chiefly at the bidding of kings, the people have found the graves of their heroes in the churchyard, have followed their ashes to the rivers where spite and malice flung them, have chanted their stories in song and set up their memorials in marble and bronze. If men of blood and ambition are the ideals of a nation, we find a nation of warriors; if patriots are the heroes, be they on the battle-field or in the council chamber, we find a nation proud of its nationality. Nor are our heroes only the leaders. A personal friend of Mr. Lincoln tells how he rode with him in a carriage through the city of Washington when its squares were dotted with camps, and its streets were full of boys in blue. When generals and field-officers saluted him, he returned the compliment by the customary and formal wave of the hand, but when a private soldier presented arms, he rose in his carriage and took off his hat. He did not undervalue leadership, but he appreciated that patriotic, unheralded support of the flag which was found in the lines. And so our people, in memorializing the critical struggle at Antietam, chose for a symbol, not a portrait of one of the many general officers who made great names on that historic ground, but the figure of an American soldier, with no state or regimental distinction, only a type of the hundreds of thousands who fought and fell, and whose names do not appear in the histories, but whose blood won the victory.

If it is true that the admiration of a community is significant of its character, it is equally true of its contempt. It is not military greatness that we honor to-day, it is loyalty to manhood and to truth and to country. When the aggressions of the mother country became insufferable, and the cry was "to arms," there were two men upon the soil of our little Connecticut, who were especially conspicuous for their military accomplishments. Both incarnated personal bravery; neither had learned an alphabet out of which the word "fear" could be made; both were leaders. One gathered the sons of New Haven upon the Green and drilled them for war,—the other left his oxen in the field and rode to Boston. Both had achieved success and glory in the earlier wars. The eyes not only of Connecticut and New England, but of Virginia and the Carolinas turned to both of them. Both were offered high places by the enemy. One went through the struggle with an unclouded story, and to-day his name, the name of Putnam, is written upon nine counties in nine states, and we are bending in reverence before his statue. The other fled his country, died in ignominy, and an American community would as soon adopt the name of Judas as the name of Arnold.

Nations are not created by acts of parliament, nor by acts of congress, nor are they made by treaties. Statutes and treaties imply states behind them. Nations grow—grow from the people. The United States are the result of no sovereignty but the sovereignty of this great people—a people made and being made of the manifold strength of the older folk. Time has winnowed away the chaff and sifted out the grain from many peoples, and many races, and has brought many good "remnants" together, to work out in wholesome friction the best methods of self-government and constitutional law. Hither have come, each with a gift, first of all and best of all, the Puritan to New England, and the sturdy Scotchman, the honest Briton, the quick-witted Irishman, the Huguenot, son of a martyr and father of heroes, the Dutchman, full of honesty and trade, the German — happy combination of much goodness and few faults, the Scandinavian, the Italian, the Mongolian, and the African, by the grace of God and the will of the people and the terrible tribulation of war, transformed from chatteldom to manhood.

In studying the history of our country, we may and must study its biographies. Its own biography, so to say, is made up of the stories of its individual lives. It was once taught, with more or less truth,

that the genius of a whole nation is the creation of
a single life, as Alexander's and Solomon's and
Julius Cæsar's. It is only a partial truth. The individual of mark represents, just as truly as he creates,
a community. Marcus Aurelius and Christopher
Columbus were not prodigies, springing from the air
or the sky or the rocks:—their roots struck into soil
—they were born in the travail of forces, which are
only lost to our sight because the chronicles were kept
by courtiers. It is a flippant philosophy which sees in
human progress only the work of individual greatness ;
the great individual incarnates in blossom and fruit,
the processes of society for an era, as the aloe expresses
the natural forces of a century. We look at the
liberal legislation of England for a quarter of a century,
its education bills, its burials bills, its extension of the
franchise, its disestablishments, and we give glory to
Gladstone and Peel. But behind Gladstone and Peel
there has been a great constituency, struggling with
burdens and pleading for rights, often in inarticulate
ways, and they have only waited for the strong arm
of Peel and the matchless voice of Gladstone to strike
and speak for them. We look back to the first half
of the seventeenth century, and we glory in Winthrop
and Hooker, but Winthrop and Hooker were largely
representative of the common ideas of the little colony.
We stand in reverence before Washington, in admiration before Trumbull, and Adams, and Hamilton, in
enthusiasm before Putnam and Moultrie, but let us
never forget the hardy, believing, self-denying men
whom they represented and who supported them.
When we honor Putnam, and Wooster, and Knowlton,
and Chester, and Humphreys, let us never forget the

thirty-one thousand, nine hundred and thirty-one men, most of them private soldiers, whom Connecticut sent to the revolutionary fields, from Ticonderoga to York-town. Neither let us forget that the atmosphere of Connecticut was charged with ozonic forces of the most patriotic and self-centered kind. Our ancient seat of learning at New Haven was a very furnace of patriotism. In 1774, Dr. (President) Stiles wrote "there is to be another Runnymede in New England." In 1779, President Napthali Daggett, with his fowling piece blazing away at British regulars, made the most picturesque single portrait of the war. And a greater than both, through the war a tutor, but afterwards President, one of America's chief educators, Timothy Dwight, whose distinguished grandson and successor to-day leads our worship of Almighty God, was firing the young men of Yale with that burning patriotism which prepared them so well for the prominent part which they were so soon to play in the trying campaigns of war. Of the small number of alumni upon Yale's catalogue in the days of the revolution, two hundred and thirty-four rendered conspicuous personal service upon the battlefield. The universities have been the friends of freedom. Bigotry and tyranny are exorcised from the human mind, as evil spirits, by the influence of intelligence and education and culture, an influence covering and blessing both the learned and the unlearned.

You will not expect an extended sketch of our hero to-day—only now and then a leaf from his life. Salem had the honor of his birth, in 1718, and well did he repay the obligations of his Massachusetts' nativity, by the defense and deliverance which he brought to her territory. He was of sturdy, English blood, and, curiously enough, the family crest was a wolf's head.

Like Washington and Hale, in his youth he was a conspicuous leader in athletic sports. When he visited the city of Boston for the first time, and his rural appearance excited uncomplimentary comment from a city youth of twice his size, who chaffed him in a way to which the country boy was not accustomed, the young Israel proceeded to amuse the Boston people, who even at that early day seem to have had a keen eye for the champion's belt, by a thorough, if not a scientific pounding of his antagonist. He was first married at twenty-one years of age, and at once moved to Pomfret. He settled at Mortlake, and became a large proprietor of land. Here, in industry and domestic virtue, he pursued the hardy life of a Connecticut farmer. He was fond of horses and was interested in stock-breeding. Here occurred the wolf's den incident, a story which will be told to reverent and admiring boys as a classic so long as boys admire pluck and bravery—which may it be as long as grass grows! In the French and Indian war, beginning as a captain under Sir William Johnson in 1753, he continued in service until his final return from Canada, in 1762.

In looking at the great deliverance from the oppressions of England in our war for independence, we are sometimes tempted to forget the importance of the earlier struggles, in which our fathers fought, as British colonists, against the aggressions of France upon the North. This contest continued at intervals for nearly a century before the revolution. The English colonists held the coast. They had brought here the free ideas of the common law, of *magna charta*, and the bill of rights. They had done much more; they had abolished primogeniture and entails, had introduced reasonable laws of inheritance, had established universal education, had made, in the cabin of the Mayflower, an embryonic attempt at a written constitution, and, at Hartford, in 1639, had indeed made a written constitution which is the type of the written constitutions·of modern civilization. They were learning the sovereignty of the individual man, and were unlearning lessons of subservience and idolatry to rank, and title, and heredities, and despotisms, and divine rights, and prelacies, and spiritual and temporal lordships, which were entrenched in Bastilles, and behind pillars of Hercules, built up by centuries on centuries of assumptions, traditions, prescriptions, and possessions, supported by credulity and superstition, by fears, natural and unnatural, by the power of money and of the sword, by punishments in the name of law and by threats of everlasting punishment in the flames of hell. Out of these bigotries and horrible oppressions of body, and mind, and soul, and into these regions of political right and moral sweetness and intellectual light, the Puritans in New England, and the colonists in Virginia and Maryland were leading a civilization better even than the advanced civilization of England. But there were other powers struggling to get possession of this fair land—little known then for its real physical worth, but at least known as a market for European wares, and as yielding something in the way of furs, and a few other articles of value. For many years French civilization on the North and West, and Anglo-Saxon civilization on the East, wrestled for supremacy. The scene of the conflict was New York and Canada, and Northern and Eastern Pennsylvania. The French held the great rivers, could make war with the Indians for allies as against the English colonists, whose course with the Indians had always been unwise and unjust, a policy which we haven't yet outgrown. In the end the flimsy Latin civilization was driven from the country, and we were delivered from the power of Bourbonism, and the hands on the dial went forward and not backward.

And what a country was then saved for the larger humanities ! A land, the granary and garden of the world, the story of whose factories and agriculture and commerce is a very miracle of progress ; a land, great in material wealth and its innumerable agencies and demonstrations of mercantile success, and even greater in its elevations of the humble, its development and culture and education of the many, its abolition of class notions and class facts in political and religious life, its loyalty to law without the defence of bayonets, and its development of that personal freedom which is the supreme Divine gift that lifts man to manhood ; a land offering to human study the sublime picture of a nation, inconceivably strong, and every year becoming stronger in geometrical progressions, according to the will of Almighty God, governing itself without the sceptre of a king, or the patronizing dominion of an enthroned ecclesiastic, or the tread and tramp of a standing army.

And this repulse of haughty Bourbon France could never have been won by the British army alone, and her Braddocks and Abercrombies. They knew little of the country and less of the hostile Indians. But the provincials knew the Indians and their ways, and they knew the country, and its mountains, and rivers, and swamps, and its winters, too.

We risk little in saying that for audacity, intrepidity, ingenuity, for an imprudence which concealed the very genius of prudence, for sagacity, intuition, prescience of hostile manœuver, for leadership in woods and boats and swamps, no single man who entered into that conflict was the superior of Israel Putnam. He was not slow in exhibiting his peculiar genius in these campaigns. He soon found out the incapacity of many of his superiors. Several times he took unauthorized responsibilities, and once or twice forbidden ones, which were only saved from severe criticism by the brilliant success which attended him on each occasion, and by the demonstrations which he so often made of his larger intelligence. As an Indian fighter, Putnam had qualifications which have not been excelled in the long story of our conflicts with the red men, from John Mason to George S. Crook. And, in the more regular contests with the Frenchmen, he was almost uniformly a successful and skilful officer. His bravery was of that highest kind which never lost its wisdom. When he and Major Rogers were examining Crown Point, and had moved up so close to the fort and so far from their troops that Rogers was taken, Putnam had no idea of letting Rogers go into captivity, nor any more idea of firing a gun to insure his own; so he knocked the captor of his friend dead with one blow from his old fusee. The career of Putnam in in these earliest wars was as romantic as the journeys and battles of Æneas, and as real as martyrdom.

In the forests and swamps and fields, in rapids and
creeks, and on the lakes, by night and by day, in re-
connoitre, or bush fight or battle line, as scout, or as
company leader, in charge of a battalion or in single
combat, he was tireless in action, fertile in expedients,
absolutely insensible to fear and almost invariably a
victor. A prisoner, bound to a tree, struck in the
jaw by the butt of a Frenchman's musket, his head
made a target for Indian tomahawks, then released
and tied to a stake, surrounded by faggots, and, when
the flames were already scorching him, rescued by
the bravery of an officer as by a miracle, his iron
nerve never failed him. Prostrate upon his back and
tied to two stout saplings at diverging angles, and
surrounded by sleeping Indians, suffering the agonies
of the rack, his humor bubbled into a laugh as he
thought what a droll picture it all would make for a
painter's canvas. He struggled with fire at the magazine for hours, until but a single thickness of board
stood between the furious element and the gunpowder,
and until he conquered, and saved fort, garrison, and
magazine, his hands and face and legs blistered and
burned, the very skin coming off with his burnt mit-
tens. There is more pluck exhibited than glory in
prospect in such a fight with fire at the very lip of a
magazine. At last, maimed, worn, and lacerated, he
arrived a prisoner at Montreal. Here he met the cul-
tured and patriotic Colonel Philip Schuyler. At the
shocking sight of Putnam's condition, Colonel
Schuyler said that it was difficult to restrain his
language "within bounds consistent with the prudence of a prisoner and the meekness of a Christian."
In this war Putnam was doing more than to

help in whipping the French. He was studying as well the strength and the weakness of the British soldier, and the qualities and invincibilities of his provincial neighbors and brethren.

For the next twelve or more years after the French and Indian war, Putnam remained at home an object of admiration and love by his neighbors and many friends. He was honored by civil office and enjoyed the hearty esteem of the colonists.

And here we claim for Putnam an intuition of the coming independence, which few, even of the most radical of the fathers, dared to hope for. A complete and successful separation and a new republic were things which great and wise leaders regarded as hardly to be desired, still less to be expected. Freedom under the crown was the general hope. But this unlettered man thought deeper and saw more clearly the struggles to come, and their issue. He waited for a war which he felt was at hand and for a victory which he felt was to be ours. He well understood the encroaching tyranny of the crown, he knew there could be but one solution of provincial troubles and in that fearful contest, with its not unguessed agonies, and sorrows, and disappointments, and jealousies, and mistakes, he knew the ultimate invincibility of the American colonists. And so, when a stamp master was appointed to enforce the stamp act in Connecticut, Putnam inspired the measures, more forcible than polite, which resulted in his resignation. And his statement to Governor Fitch on the subject was so unmistakable in its tenor that no stamps ever came to this colony from New York. When the Port bill oppressed Boston, Putnam sent on sheep and lambs, and openly declared that their blood was but a type of the sacrifice which he and his neighbors were ready to make in the common defence. And when the tidings of Lexington came, the old prophet saw the morning in whose twilight he had been watching. Even the accomplished Warren, upon whose green grave the muses of history and poetry and eloquence have delighted to linger, no less a patriot than Putnam, but more conservative, and inclined to hope yet in the power of persuasion, and perhaps trusting to the noble oratory of Chatham, failed to convince the blunt old soldier that harmony was possible, and ultimately acquiesced in his bold measures. When British officers reasoned with him on the folly of colonial resistance, and asked him if he had any doubt that five thousand veterans could march through the continent, "no doubt," said he, "if they behaved civilly and paid well for everything they wanted;" "but," he continued, after a pause, "if in an hostile manner, though the American men were out of the question, the women with ladles and broomsticks would knock them all on the head before they could get half through." Putnam expected to fight the mother country and expected to win.

For these intuitions we claim eminence for our General. It is given to few to feel the first waters of tides, to know the gathering storms and coming sun bursts, to measure the patience and endurance of peoples in the shadow of death, and to forecast the issues of crises, as by instinct. Such power of insight we conceive was the highest trait in the composition of that peculiar man, Abraham Lincoln. Such

powers normally belong to men of the people. Here
kings and prelates have often failed. Putnam was
thoroughly of the people. His call to the Major
Generalship was by a *vox populi*, which stood not
upon proprieties of order in promotion. Untrained
in letters, the wants of his countrymen and their
rights had been his alphabet. He had found out the
capacities for endurance of man's physical nature,
the inborn sovereignty of the people, the electric
power of patriotism. And so he looked across the
ocean to the King and felt the certain comings of
continued and increasing exactions; he looked over
the rough hills of New England, and the plains of
the South, and from Lake Champlain to Georgia he
heard the speech of patriots and their prayers, and, as
clearly as he foresaw the snows of December and the
foliage of June, he recognized the coming clash of
arms and the deliverance of the oppressed.

The call came soon. It found him in the field.
Leaving his oxen unloosed and mounting his horse,
he rode to Boston to the fight which he saw had
come, and had come to stay until it should be forever
settled upon principles of freedom and right. He
forsook his home and the joys of domestic life to
serve the people without a hesitating look or word.
He returned from Massachusetts for troops, and was
appointed a General by Connecticut.

It was but a few weeks from Lexington to
Bunker Hill.

"God helps the heavy battalions," said Napo-
leon. God helped David and his sling, says history.
Is it to be a victory for Napoleonism, and the fire of
hell which he made the genius and motive of battle,

or shall wrath and its remainders be turned to praise and made to promote the ongoings of truth and the civilization of society?

It was a sorry match as a military problem. Here were regulars, veterans, victors of many fields, trained to touch shoulders, to hear commands, to march and wheel in time; their arms were well appointed and clean, their ammunition was plentiful and of the best; their officers were educated, experienced, brave. Here were traditions, and prestige, and the grip of the leading monarchy of the world upon its colonies. Here were ships of war and the flames of fire striking terror by the horrors of a burning city. But here too, were tyranny, and oppression, and pride, and swelling self-confidence.

There were a few hundred yeomen with insufficient arms and ·short rounds of powder and shot. They have come from Massachusetts, and Connecticut, and New Hampshire. Their leaders have had little council together. They have scraped up a clumsy redoubt and have covered a rail fence with loose hay. Thank God they are on a hill! But if they are awkward, untried soldiers, they are freeholders and freemen. If they have no common acquaintance, they have a common cause; if they have no uniformity of dress or of arms, they have but one purpose and a single inspiration. If they have left different firesides in different states, they have all left homes with kindred watch-words. They all love freedom and God; they all hate oppression and the King. And with them and over them are invisible things in holy concert; the elevation of man, the supremacy of constitutional law, the transfiguration of human beings from vassalage to independence, and the will of Almighty God that these vast millions of acres of land, and lake, and river, with treasures unguessed of soil, and stream, and mine, shall not be tributary to the haughty little island across the Atlantic.

The assault was made, and renewed, and again renewed. The people watched the struggle from the roofs and steeples of Boston, and held up the cause of the patriots with their prayers. And the friends of man have returned to the picture of that struggle again and again, and with tears of joy. The undisciplined yeomanry withstood the charge of the best disciplined troops, and the crowning victory of Yorktown was spoken from Bunker Hill. The last of the retiring patriots, he who had filled, as nearly as the circumstances would allow anyone to fill it, the position of commanding general, who had superintended the construction of the humble fortifications, who had cautioned the patriots to hold their fire and to husband their powder, who had offered his stalwart body as a target for British balls from the beginning to the end, upon the hill, in the field, and in the highway, in the assault, in urging reinforcements, and in the final withdrawal, was Israel Putnam.

Three weeks after the battle Samuel B. Webb wrote from the seat of war at Cambridge:

" You will find that Generals Washington and Lee are vastly prouder and think higher of Putnam than of any man in the army, and he, truly, is the hero of the day."

On the 9th of July, 1775, Silas Deane, a Connecticut man of national reputation and intensely patriotic, wrote from Philadelphia, then the capital city:

" The cry here is Connecticut forever. So high has the universally applauded conduct of our Governor (Trumbull), and the brave intrepidity of old General Putnam and his troops raised our colony in the estimation of the whole continent." And again on July 20th, 1775, he writes:

" Putnam's merit runs through the continent; his fame still increases, and every day justifies the unanimous applause of the country. Let it be remembered that he had every vote of the congress for Major-General, and his health has been the second or third at almost all our tables in this city."

But they were all heroes. Not only Putnam, and Prescott, and Warren, and Stark, and Knowlton, and Chester, and Grosvenor, but each one of the fifteen hundred who proved in the heat and carnage of that June afternoon that free hearts are invincible. On the 17th of June, 1775, Artemas Ward and Charles Lee were chosen to the office of Major-General by congress, and on the 19th of June, Philip Schuyler and Israel Putnam were elected to the same rank, and of the four, Putnam alone was chosen unanimously.

I have alluded to Putnam as the commanding officer at Bunker Hill. It is enough to say that the voice of contemporaneous literature and the representations of the early sketches and pictures of the battle as published in this country and on the other side of the ocean, are substantially unanimous in demonstration of the fact. It was reserved for later and ill-judged criticism to question it. The artificial rules of etiquette and precedence were then, as they had been before, and as they now are, and as they ever will be, the cause of historical quarrel and discussion. The

troops about Boston had their own State com-
manders; indeed, Major Stark, of New Hampshire,
was chosen to his rank by the soldiers upon the
ground. There was little unity of plan. General
Ward, who was the officer in command of all the
forces, was at Cambridge. It is almost certain that
General Putnam represented him at the battle, but the
troops on the hill were chiefly from Massachusetts,
and the Massachusetts troops were in the redoubt
where Colonel Prescott had personal command. It
is a fair statement of the case to say that Putnam's
rank gave him the command by his presence on the
field; that the plan of the engagement and its execu-
tion were principally his, although he was unable to
get the reinforcements which were needed and for
which he made loud demand and continued exertion.
In the broad sense of leadership there can be no
doubt in any impartial mind that he was the leader of
the American troops, and was so considered by friends
and foes at the day and time.

It is to be regretted that doubts about Putnam's
capacity for leadership, and even about his courage,
have been raised, but they must have been. They
were raised about Washington, and Greene, and every
great leader in the revolution. And one only needs
to read any history, so called, to see the strange possi-
bilities of conclusion to which authorities can arrive in
their accounts of battles, and estimates of military
men and military affairs. Nor is this peculiarity of
historical literature exclusively true of the battle-
field. It has been several times argued, and last of
all by the mysterious language of ciphers, by which
any literary result conceivable can be attained, that

the greatest of poets and dramatists did not write his own plays, and, still later, we learn that the most charming, characteristic, and inimitable reminiscence of a great war, written by our own greatest soldier and greatest man, was, in fact, the literary achievement of another, whose greatness the Republic had failed to appreciate. But while it is true, such is the power of partisanship, prepossession, and bias over the human mind, and so easily do we make into beliefs those thoughts which are born of our wishes, that there can be few facts of history which, in a quarter of a century after their occurrence, will not be questioned, the world will still justly credit Hamlet to Shakespeare, his Memoirs to Grant, and Bunker Hill to Putnam.

Washington did not meet Putnam until he came to Cambridge. They had both achieved glory in the Indian war; they knew and loved each other, but they met for the first time at the headquarters of the Continental army. And the absolute confidence which Washington had in Putnam never abated until death. He had no doubt about delivering his Major-General's commission to him with his own hands, while he hesitated in the case of others. He had no doubt in sending him to New York to take chief command, after the enemy had retreated from Boston, and after Putnam himself had taken possession of the forts, provisions, guns, stores, and supplies in the name of the thirteen colonies. He had no doubt in intrusting to him the supreme command at Philadelphia in his own absence. He had no doubt in directing him to open his military letters. He had no doubt of his purity, patriotism, and rare capacity,

.

when he addressed him in words of deep tenderness,
in the day of an assured peace based upon our
national independence.

The story of Putnam's career from Bunker
Hill until his paralysis in the winter of 1779–80
is deeply interesting. He had his share, and no
more, of the ill fortunes of the campaigns, and
he had his full share of success. He fought the
so-called battle of Long Island under circumstances
for which he was not responsible, but which made
success impossible; he conducted the retreat through
the present limits of the City of New York before the
superior force of Lord Howe with characteristic fear-
lessness and courage. His discriminating eye selected the heights of West Point as a base of oper-
ations; he captured hundreds, probably thousands, of
prisoners in the Jerseys; he beat the bullets of the
British dragoons as he rode down Horseneck steps,
where no red coat dared to follow him, and so
aroused the admiration and wonder of Gov. Tryon,
of odious memory, that he sent him a new cap for
the one which had been ventilated by a British musket ball. He replied to the haughty demand of
British officers for the return of the spy, Edmund
Palmer, in such accurate and concise terms, that the
letter has passed into classic literature.

It was not to be that Putnam's voice should
thunder commands and his sword flash in the
final victories. The horrible shock of his captivity in the earlier war, the re-action from his
wearied life of exposure, the strain of his long
ride to Concord and Boston, as glorious and
heroic as Paul Revere's, had searched through the

joints of even his matchless harness. As he was
on his way to headquarters, at sixty-one years of age,
the wild throbs of his noble heart pressed too sorely
upon his aching brain, and the strong man fell; those
muscles, which never before had refused to obey the
commands of his sovereign will, gave no response.
It was a sad ride back to his loved Mortlake, and the
fields which he had made green, and the flocks which
he had guarded, and the friends for whom he had
long hazarded his life. But it was to be. He must
wait, with moist eyes and lifted prayer, for the good
end of whose coming he made no doubt. For eleven
years, with unclouded mind, until the surrender of
Cornwallis, and the final peace, and the recognition
of the union by the European nations, and the
adoption of the constitution, and the oath of the first
President, watched by admiring friends, telling over
and over again the adventures and victories of the
past, he lived close to the spot where he now sleeps,
until the 29th of May, 1790, when he went on to join
the patriot Governor, Jonathan Trumbull, and the
patriot martyr, Nathan Hale, and to wait awhile to
welcome Washington and LaFayette.

Think not as you read of Putnam's bravery that
it was the bravery of thoughtlessness; his courage
was of the kind that thinks. Think not, as you see
him soiled in the grime of battle and red with blood
stains, that he rejoiced in destruction; he was as
sensitive to the sufferings of others as a mother.
Think not as you study his rugged features that he
was vulgar and brutal, he guarded the honor of
woman with the chivalry of a knight. Think not as
you hear him hiss imprecations, in his lisping accent,

upon the British troops, that he was a blasphemer; so were their enemies cursed by the devout Hebrew prophets and psalmists, whose battle hymns Putnam studied as models inspired from heaven. Think not he loved war more than peace, the battle-field more than the farm, the camp more than home. He loved war for the sake of peace and freedom, he loved the battle-field because he loved his farm, he loved the camp because he saw through and beyond its tents the rest of home.

Let us never for a moment believe that the fathers fought for military glory or for war's sake. They fought for peace and for law; for states which they loved and for a Union whose future they but dimly guessed. Indeed when the war was over, and the independence of the United States was assured, and the representatives of the states were convened to form a constitution, how little did even they know in what supreme architecture they were building, and how great things they were creating. There has never been assembled in the history of the world, in the name of country, or science, or religion, a company of men of like numbers, who brought to their duties larger intellectual capacity, and higher moral qualities and purer patriotism, nor one that was more apparently under the special guidance of the great Father of all men, than the little band of statesmen which met in Philadelphia to organize a constitution for the people of the thirteen confederated states. And Connecticut was there by a representation inferior to none—by Sherman, second only to Franklin in wisdom, by Ellsworth, unsurpassed in eloquence, and by Johnson, unexcelled in scholarship. As to-day we have a lineal descendant of President Dwight to lead our devotions, so are we fortunate in having a lineal descendant of Dr. William Samuel Johnson to sound the rhythm of our verses.

In passing, let me remind you that our Connecticut Sherman was the only man who enjoys the singular place in history of having signed the four supreme papers of American independence: the Articles of Association of the congress of 1774, the Articles of Confederation, the Declaration of Independence, and the Constitution.

Had that little body of men really felt the full greatness of their work, for themselves and their children, for the American people, and for humanity, they must have risen above their environment to heights of seership never before scaled. With local attachments, strong and dominant, and yet bound together by the success of a union against oppression, and conscious of the weakness of a confederation which had no element of nationality in it, they wrought out that matchless instrument which reserved to the several communities self-government in the matters which are best left to local control, and bound a people into unity in those matters which make a nation for national defense, and national commerce, and national welfare. The rights of the states are safest in the sovereignty of the nation, and the nationality of the Republic is safest in the self-government of the states. So are the waves distinct, but it is one sea; so are the trees distinct, but it is one forest; so are the mountains distinct, but it is one range. And the older nations are copying more and

more our example of home rule in local matters, and
national control in national things, and the will of
the people, limited only by the solemn, catholic,
unimpassioned principles of organic law, supreme in
each.

As we recall the history of the fathers, reverence
and gratitude bid us bend at many a battle field and
in many a council chamber. And how often are we
tempted to say of this or that or the other one, that
his strong arm, or his heart's blood, or his foresight,
or his patience, or his genius at harmonizing discord,
or his zeal of enthusiasm, or his inspiring magnetism,
or his clarion word of command, or his silent act of
obedience, was the salvation of the young nation, as
it escaped destruction in ten thousand crises!

But it is neither easy, nor wise, nor necessary to
separate too sharply the greatness of the revolutionary heroes into its individual forces. It is seldom
that nature resolves her shafts of light into prismatic
colors and writes their elemental hues upon the sky.
The dash of Wayne, the daring of Putnam, the tireless strategy of Greene on the field, the wisdom of
Trumbull, the courageous and tenacious counsel of
Adams and Quincy, the eloquence of Ellsworth, the
sagacity of Franklin and Sherman, the genius of
Hamilton, and the foresight of Morris, in the state,
and the supreme and unique judgment, patriotism,
and leadership, both on the field and in the state, of
the one and only Washington were all blended in
the harmonies of a historic whole which has bathed
humanity with a flood of light leading on toward a
perfect day.

Putnam was not learned in martial lore, he was
8

not a master of the alleged chess-board of war; he was not a combiner of great military causes to bring about great strategic results. In managing divisions, corps, and brigades, in distributions of the different arms of the service, artillery, cavalry, infantry, commissary, and hospital, in generalizations of campaigns, or of a single battlefield, he was surpassed by many of his revolutionary associates — by many, whose commissions ran out for one cause or another before the end — as well as by Washington and Greene. Like Wayne and Arnold, he fought whatever was in front of him; battle-line, fortress, bushman, hostile boats, white man, black man, red man — if it hindered his cause, if it stayed his advance, it must go away or go down. He believed in hard pounding in attack, so did Wellington and Grant. He was fertile in plan within certain ranges, and could fight the fire of stratagem with the fire of counter stratagem. Like Grant again, he moved very early in the morning, and like that same great general and greater man, he never learned that there was a time to quit the field while a ray of light flamed in the sky. He was a military leader rather than a great general. His leadership was marked by enthusiasm and faith, by daring and tenacity and endurance. And he was in every fibre of his being a true man — kind, honest, pure, conscientious, devout. He loved goodness, and good men, and good things; he hated jealousies, and envies, and bitterness, and injustice.

Putnam was not a scholar; he knew nothing of the dead languages of Virgil and Herodotus, but he needed no pedagogue to translate for him the legend "E pluribus unum," nor clerkly minister to interpret for him the motto "Qui transtulit sustinet." He was unfamiliar with the written philosophies of state craft, but he knew that freemen were competent to make a state without the consent of a king. He knew nothing of navigation, but when duty called him to descend the rapids of the Hudson, he found a new course through boiling waves, and past sharp edged rocks. He knew little about the scientific distinction between original and reflected light, and he never heard of the spectroscope, but he knew that the moonlight on the river was his ally to scourge the treacherous Indians. He had never heard of evolution nor studied the birth of nations, but out of the travails of campaigns in Canada, and bitter suffering by Lake Champlain, by the stone walls of Lexington, and the hay-fence ramparts of Bunker Hill, he felt the certain birth of an independent nation at that early hour, when even the great Washington and Adams only dared to hope for a better and more honorable dependence upon the mother country. The fibres of his being were neither by nature nor by culture delicate or refined, but his heart beat and his nerves thrilled with a patriotism as pure and true as the on-rushing waters of Niagara. If there was no place in his garden for tropical flowers, there was no room there for poisonous grasses. If he had little conception of the great universe of stars and planets, he knew there was to be a new day, and he stood and waited for the dawn with his sword in hand.

What went ye out into the wilderness to see? a reed shaken with the wind?

But what went ye out into the wilderness to see? a man clothed in soft raiment? Behold they that wear soft clothing are in king's houses.

But what went ye out to see? a prophet? Yea, I say unto you and more than a prophet.

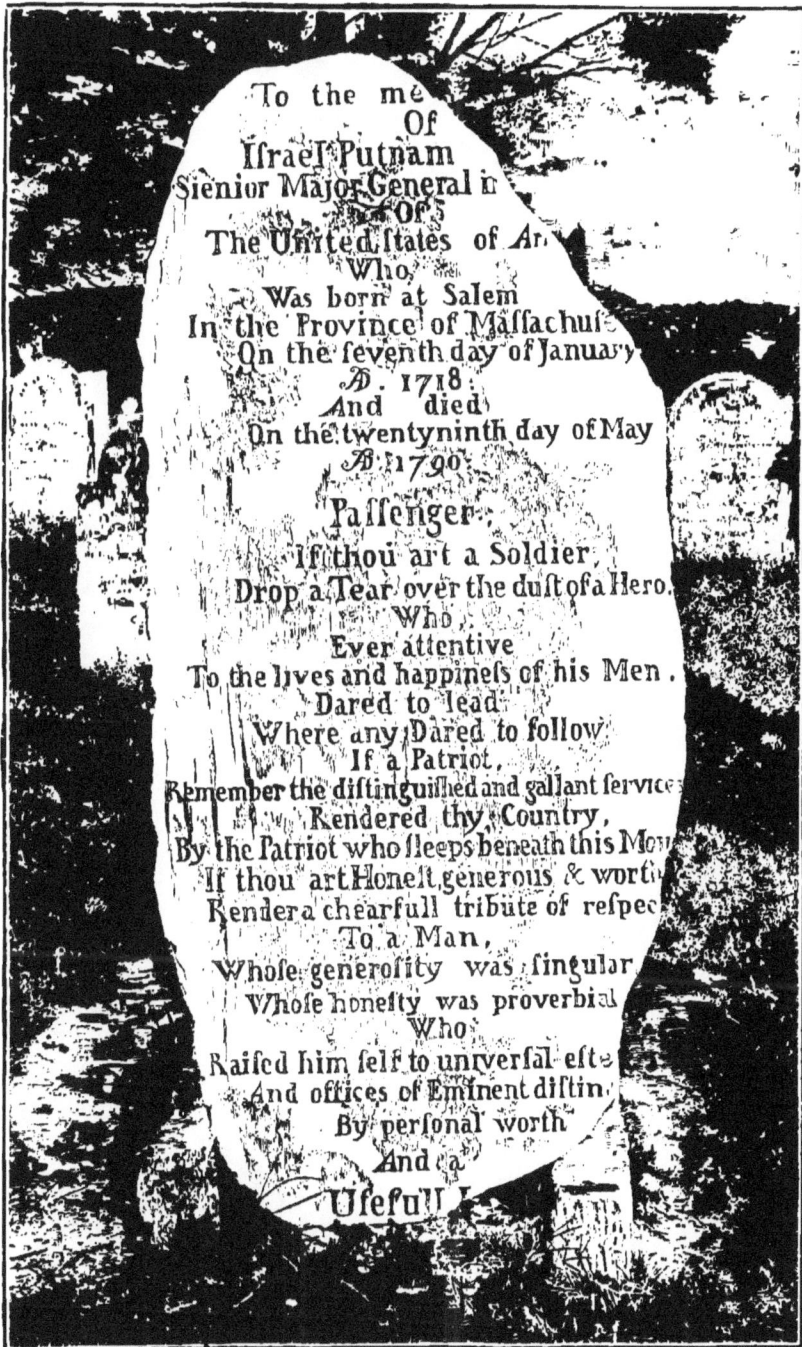

SLAB TAKEN FROM PUTNAM'S GRAVE IN BROOKLYN, AND NOW IN THE POSSESSION OF THE CONNECTICUT HISTORICAL SOCIETY.

MILITARY REVIEW.

Under command of Chief Marshal Tyler the military organization marched before Gov. Lounsbury in the following order :

First Division — Col. Havens.
Third Connecticut Regiment.
Putnam Phalanx.
First Company Governor's Foot Guard.
Second Division — Gen. D. W. Wardrop.
Montgomery Light Guard Veterans, Boston.
Roxbury Artillery, Roxbury, Mass.
Third Division — Col. Clark.
Providence (R. I.) Light Infantry.
Bristol (R. I.) Artillery.
Fourth Division — Col. C. T. Homer.
Veterans of Seventh Regiment, New York.
Veterans of Twenty-second Regiment, New York.
Veterans of Thirteenth Regiment, New York.
Veterans of Ninth Regiment, New York.
Veterans of Twenty-third Regiment, New York.
Veterans of Seventy-first Regiment, New York.

ORDER OF EXERCISES AS ARRANGED BY THE COMMISSION.

PRAYER OF INVOCATION, Rev. TIMOTHY DWIGHT, S.T.D., LL.D.
MUSIC, "HAIL COLUMBIA," BAND AND CHORUS.
PRESENTATION OF STATUE, in behalf of the Commission.
Hon. MORRIS W. SEYMOUR.

SALUTE.

ACCEPTANCE, in behalf of the State,
His Excellency, PHINEAS C. LOUNSBURY.
MUSIC, "STAR SPANGLED BANNER," BAND AND CHORUS.
POEM, Prof. CHAS. F. JOHNSON, Trinity College.
MEMORIAL ADDRESS, Hon. HENRY C. ROBINSON.
MUSIC, "AMERICA," BAND AND CHORUS.
MILITARY REVIEW, By GOVERNOR LOUNSBURY.

ITEMS OF INTEREST.

The Commissioners regret that the language of the prayer of invocation could not be secured for this report.

At the close of Mr. Seymour's remarks the statue was unveiled by John D. Putnam of Wisconsin, a great-great-grandson of Israel Putnam.

At the conclusion of the exercises announced by the Commission, Colonel Gates, of the Thirteenth New York Veterans, presented to the Commission a floral design of great beauty, representing the corps badge of the association.

Governor Taft of Rhode Island, in response to the hearty greetings of the spectators, spoke as follows :

MR. CHAIRMAN AND GENTLEMEN :

I am glad to be present on this occasion, to respond briefly for the State of Rhode Island; for we have gathered here to pay respect to the memory of one who occupied a large place in the minds and hearts of the whole people during that struggle from which sprang the birth of a nation.

The State I represent was a participant in that contest, and furnished men who left behind the memory of their glorious deeds. General Nathaniel Greene was no less illustrious than his companion in arms, General Israel Putnam, whose memory we this day commemorate. No monument has been erected in Rhode Island to him who fought by the side of Connecticut's hero, other than that in the hearts of her people. I trust the day is not far distant when you may be asked to participate in the dedication of one similar to that before us, made from enduring bronze and granite, erected to the memory of General Nathaniel Greene, Rhode Island's greatest son.

Mr. Wm. H. Putnam, only surviving grandson of Israel Putnam, Mr. Gerhardt, the sculptor, and Mr. Thos. S. Marlor, the generous citizen of Brooklyn, were called to the front of the platform by President Seymour, where they were honored with approving cheers by the assembled soldiers and civilians.

The following is the famous inscription written by President Dwight shortly after Putnam's death, for the tombstone at Brooklyn, and now inscribed on the pedestal of the statue :

Sacred be this Monument
•   to the memory
of
Israel Putnam, Esquire,
Senior Major General in the Armies
of
the United States of America,
who
was born at Salem,
in the Province of Massachusetts,
on the 7th day of January,
A. D. 1718.
and died
on the 20th day of May,
A. D. 1790.
Passenger,
If thou art a soldier,
drop a tear over the dust of a Hero
who
ever attentive
to the lives and happiness of his men,
dared to lead
where any dared to follow;
if a Patriot,
remember the distinguished and gallant
services rendered thy country
by the Patriot who sleeps beneath this marble; if thou art honest, generous
and worthy, render a cheerful tribute of respect
to a man
whose generosity was singular,
whose honesty was proverbial;
who
raised himself to universal esteem,
and offices of eminent distinction,
by personal worth
and a
useful life.

The Commissioners desire to express their earnest appreciation of the kind assistance received from the citizens and choir of Brooklyn, the Putnam Phalanx, and the patriotic press of Connecticut.

They desire also to extend special thanks to the distinguished authors of the literary exercises that form the valuable part of this history, and they feel it their duty to say of Mr. Robinson that he consented to deliver the memorial address only because his associates would not listen to his repeated refusals to do so.

The generous words that have already been spoken in praise of the statue are due to the sculptor and the State.

The Commissioners will be satisfied if it shall be said that their efforts have indirectly resulted in calling again to the stirrup the man who watched with Washington the cradle of the new-born nation, until the daring words that had been traced by Jefferson in fading ink were rewritten in crimson letters on the scattered tents of monarchy.

GEO. P. McLEAN,
In behalf of the Commissioners.

www.ingramcontent.com/pod-product-compliance
Lightning Source LLC
Chambersburg PA
CBHW021530270326
41930CB00008B/1174